Charisma Improvement

Improve Your Social and Communication Skills, Increase Your Self-Confidence, Influence People and Learn the Art of Public Speaking

Table of Contents

Introduction

Congratulations on purchasing *Charisma Improvement: Improve Your Social and Communication Skills, Increase Your Self-Confidence, Influence People, and Learn the Art of Public Speaking.* Thank you for doing so.

The following chapters will discuss the power of charisma and how to command respect and get the attention of everyone without having to do so much. In this book, you are going to learn how to be an excellent public speaker and how to gain a presence anywhere you find yourself.

The 21st century is fast becoming occupied with smart things and smart people who pay more attention to gadgets than they do to people. Apart from that, the world is becoming a complicated place—we can blame it on the busy activities everyone strives to meet up with and the goals we have all set for ourselves.

In the face of the emerging world, the lies need to be heard. Indeed, everyone has a voice, but not every voice commands presence and screams for attention. If you have ever stood to address a crowd, you will know how difficult it is to control the attention of an audience.

Have you ever been in a room with a lot of people, and someone walks in to steal the glare and steer of everyone in the room? Why was the same attention given to every other person that walked into the same room? The answer is not in the beauty of the person because the chances are that there are other beautiful people in the room but lie in the person's charisma. Somehow, some people can command a certain level of charisma that can't be easily matched.

How then can everyone command such charisma, and what are the things that characterize a charismatic person? Is it possible to speak to people and have them listen to you regardless of whatever form of distraction there maybe? All these and more are the things you will find in this book. There are plenty of books on this subject, thanks again for choosing this one! Every effort was made to ensure it is full of as much useful information as possible, and please enjoy it!

Chapter 1: Overview of Charisma

Everyone talks about charisma and how they want to have it so badly. But what really is the word charisma? When you think of famous people and role models, you will refer to them as being charismatic. The synonyms for charisma are captivating, alluring, charming, fascinating, bewitching, enchanting, seductive, and magnetic. With all these powerful words to explain it, who wouldn't want to be a charismatic person? Charisma can be used for either good or bad, depending on the person that possesses it. When it's used for good, the end result is always a good feeling. Now, back to the question, what really is charisma?

What is Charisma?

Charisma is the ability of a person to attract, captivate, and impact the people that are around him/her. Most times, it is easy to note a person who has charisma; other times, it is not. To categorically say the skills or the qualities of a charismatic person can be a bit hard when it comes to comparing them with other people who are less charismatic. In this sense, it becomes difficult to say what those who are not charismatic lack.

To further define charisma, it becomes a bit more complicated because there are different categories of charismatic people. Some categories of charismatic people are usually calm and depend on their charms, rather than their words to influence people. Another type of charismatic people are those who are excellent and passionate communicators. With the kind of enthusiasm they display when they are talking, it is easy for them to sweep people off their feet.

Generally, charisma can be said to be a product of excellent communication as well as interpersonal skills. This points us to the fact that a person can easily boost his or her charisma if they want to. People usually make the mistake of thinking that charisma is something a person is born with. This isn't entirely true because it is an attribute that does not have to be innate. Charisma is learnable when you practice and with reinforcement over time.

Characteristics of a Charismatic People

Those who are charismatic are undoubtedly the most successful people in the world. Professor Wiseman, a scholar at the University of Hertfordshire, says that charisma comprises of 50% of a person's innate abilities and 50% of his learned attributes. Typically, the essential qualities of charisma are those easy actions that become a part of a person's personality. These actions also boost a person's relationship with all of those around him/her. This goes a long way to improve a person's level of satisfaction with life. Below are some of the qualities of a charismatic person. When you see someone having these qualities, you can say the person possesses charisma.

They are Good Listeners

Charismatic people are good listeners. When they listen to others, they pay undivided attention to them. A good listener will not pay mind to distractions and will not check his phone more than necessary during a conversation, and better still, they will not check it at all. Generally, people who can listen actively will hardly misunderstand others. The fact that they are good listeners makes it easy for others to speak to and confide in them. Being an active listener will make communication with people around easier, regardless of whatever position they occupy. People see active listeners as good people.

They Speak with Clarity

Charismatic person ponders on everything they are going to say before they say them and always avoid using unnecessary fillers when they speak, as this will make their speech more understandable. This is even truer with scenarios where they have to address a big audience, or when they are talking to people, they are not very familiar with. Before they speak, they rehearse the approach they are going to take. Think about it, do you need to say everything that you intend to say? What is the objective or purpose of the speech you are about to say? All these will help them stay calm, collected, and concise when they speak.

They Wear A Genuine Smile

When you give a genuine smile that comes from the most authentic parts of you, it will reflect on the outside. There is something called the *"Duchenne smile."* This is the type of smile that you literarily wear on your eyes and mouth. Being charismatic doesn't suggest they have to go everywhere with a grin, but every time they smile on the inside, people find them more attractive, and they become more receptive too.

At the University of California, Berkley, there was a study carried out on 141 senior high school class photos from the yearbook of the 1960 set of Mills College. There was a follow up on these students until they clocked 27, 43, and 52. The follow-up revealed that the women who wore Duchene smile were more likely to be married, and they also remained married while those who didn't have the smile were not successful with marriage. Those with the Duchene smile were also more likely to have a greater sense of fulfillment. By carrying out a 30 year follow up, it was discovered that this result remained consistent. It was also discovered that there was no connection between appearance and satisfaction in life as satisfaction is something that comes from within; hence, it cannot be judged from the outside.

If you can smile from your heart and can match it up with a kind personality, you will be able to receive more and also give more than you ever thought you could.

They Stand Up Tall

Charismatic people think of themselves as one whom spring runs from their navel to the head and tied to the ceiling. This is a trick that is used by dancers, and it always works so well for everyone. It helps people to maintain a good posture for the rest of their days. With a good posture, they look like a confident person who is devoid of insecurities. Although they may not be feeling that confident every day, they always have to make sure they wear that confident look. While they carry their head high, they make sure their shoulders are down and of course, their back straight.

They Always Give Praise

People always say that it is not about what a person says, but the way he says it, and this is very true. If they have to criticize another person, they take a moment to put themselves in the person's position and consider the way they would be critiqued. If they are going to criticize, they are always direct by going straight to the problem at hand. Proffer a solution and seek feedback. They also initiate a timeframe.

You will see them giving credits and compliments where they have to. They make others feel important every time they do something deserving commendation. They can even do this by complimenting someone else for a project they have just completed or a presentation that they did, which went well. It is imperative they build confidence in themselves, but they are only considered a charismatic person when they can build confidence in other people too.

They Always Remember People's Names

Our name is our unique identity and the sweetest thing for us to hear. This is a straightforward phenomenon that is important. Whenever a person tells a charismatic person his/her name, they always try to repeat it to the person. For example, by saying *"good day, Helen"* or *"it's a pleasure to meet you, Helen."* This creates an impact, especially when they mention the person's name at the end of their conversation.

They Make Eye Contacts

A charismatic person never fails to make eye contact when they are in a conversation with someone else. This is one of the essential features of a great conversation/communication. Eye contact helps a person to figure out whether or not what he is saying is getting across. With eye contact, the person you are talking to will be focused on you, and you will be focused on the words of the other person and the meaning of the other person's words. During a presentation or a speech, they make eye contact with every member of the audience at the same time. By doing this, their audience will have a sense of involvement in the event.

The above characteristics are what charismatic people possess. Some people are born with natural charisma, while others can work on their charisma and actually develop it. As you read further, you will learn the elements of charisma and how you can improve your charisma.

Chapter 2: Elements of Charisma

Regardless of your situation and your aims as a person, one of the essential requirements for success in life is the charisma of an individual. This is the quality that will enable you to have full command of a room and also endear other people to you. This is what will also convince other people of the ideas you have. Every leader who has been able to win the love and admiration of devoted followers possess charisma.

Charisma is the attribute that makes other people go unimaginable lengths for you willingly. Charismatic people are described as those that are not only powerful but are also likable. They are unique, irresistible, and possess every combination that will help them open doors of opportunities.

For some people, charisma as quality may seem like a mystery. These are the kind of people that think some people are born with charisma while others are not. Well, thankfully, this isn't the case. If you wish to develop charisma, you do not have to possess unique genes to build yourself to become a person who has an endearing, powerful, and likable demeanor.

As a result of the fact that charisma is not a magical trait that one cannot easily explain, it can be further broken down to a set of solid and generally nonverbal attitudes that a person can learn, practice, and turn into an attitude as well as a way of life. These attributes are divided into three different categories which are Presence, Power, and Warmth. When a person combines these behaviors effectively, it will result in a strong personal attribute that will attract other people to him or her.

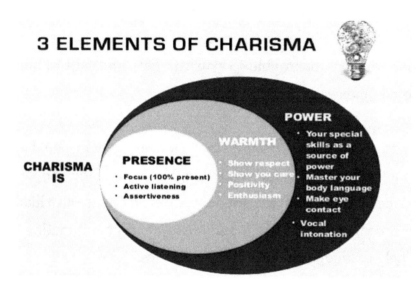

Presence

Have you ever been in a situation where you were talking to someone, but you feel like they are not paying full attention to you? Now how did you feel when you came to that realization? Angry right? Well, it's only natural for you to feel that way. It is quite unfortunate that it is only a few people that can maintain full presence when they are in conversation with other people. This has always been a challenge for so many people for the sole reason that most people have an element of conversational narcissism in them.

It gets even harder with the amount of influence that smartphones have over people in the 21st century. People now struggle to shuffle their attention between the virtual world and the real world. These days, people tend to be only physically present while their attention is with the internet world, which they fully interact with via their phones. If you walk into a restaurant, you will find people who are seated and are staring into their phones while someone else is seated across the table, but they are not conversing with each other. How funny; the world is indeed becoming a crazy place.

The good news lies in the fact that it is possible for an individual to pull himself from the world of the internet by maintaining a presence with the people that are present with them, giving them their unreserved attention.

When you think of being a charismatic person, you should consider the possibility of making yourself look like an awesome person to other people. The flip side of this quality is that you do not have to sing praises of your unique qualities. The focus should be on making other people feel welcomed and important as they are talking to you and after they have finished interacting with you. You should be able to make them feel good about themselves, much more than they did before they got into the conversation with you.

By investing a large chunk of your mental and your emotional energy on the person you are interacting with, you will be able to create an air of importance and confidence for the other person. Most of the time, what people want is attention, recognition, and acknowledgment.

To put your charisma on display, you don't have to be an outgoing person or an extrovert. Famous technology entrepreneur Elon Musk is often cited as an example of a person who has been able to gain a full grasp of the art of a charismatic presence. Elon Musk is described as an intelligent, very reserved, and quiet person by nature, but he is able to maintain a balance between his introverted nature and a good sense of focus, as well as his presence. This type of person does not need to be all out or be the life of the party to endear people to himself. He would instead concentrate on giving his full, unreserved attention to few people, than being everywhere and around everyone, chatting with them and giving a bit of himself to most of those present at the party. By giving intense attention to a few people, he makes them feel very special. In this case, what charisma offers is not quantity, but quality.

Being able to maintain presence is a simple thing to do, but most times, people find themselves struggling with achieving it. It is not something that can be faked. When you are pretending to be interested in a conversation, it is usually effortless to figure out. If you must be present, you must do so in deed and truth. This is going to demand a lot of willpower to sieve through distractions and place your attention on what the other person has to offer at a particular moment. Just like every other thing in life, it becomes easier to master with time.

Here are some tips to guide you in the art of mastering charismatic presence:

Bring Yourself to the Moment (Mindfulness)

The cradle of presence is in mind. Whenever you are in a conversation with someone, and you feel like your mind may have wandered off somewhere else, you can consider practicing mindfulness exercises to help you bring back your attention to the moment. You should pay attention to those physical sensations of your body that you always easily ignore. This may either be your breath or the feeling that comes with your feet touching the floor. You don't need long hours of meditation on these feelings. You only need a few seconds to return you to the moment that you are currently sharing with the other person.

Ensure That You Are Physically Comfortable

Bringing yourself to be physically present with a person is hard when everything that is going through your mind is how you are so uncomfortable with the shoe you are wearing or how you are not able to sit up because your tight pants may just get ripped off.

This is why you need to be as comfortable as possible. Always wear clothes that are very comfortable and well fitted. Besides the fact that it will make you feel at peace with yourself, well-fitted clothes will also make you look better. You can also increase your physical comfort by getting adequate sleep or staying away from caffeine; it is better to be calm than to be jittery.

Place Your Mobile Devices on Silence or Put Them Away

This trick has two effects: first, it will help you to avoid the temptation of checking them while you are talking to someone else. Secondly, it will make the person you are talking to know they have your undivided attention and that you are not sharing the time you have with them with your phone. This makes them feel important and would also give you all their attention.

Look at the Person You Are Talking to In the Eye

Several studies have revealed that those who make more eye contact with their audience are thought to have a lot of positive qualities. These qualities include warmth, competence, emotional stability, confidence, sincerity, and honesty. Eye contact does not only help you look appealing to the person you are talking to in every way, but it also boosts the quality of the conversation you are having. With eye contact, there is an increased sense of intimacy in your interactions, and the person who is on the other side will have a sense of positivity towards the exchange; hence, they will feel like they are connected to you in some ways.

You have to note that eye contact may work in helping you to build intimacy with friends, and in other friendly scenarios. However, research has shown that this may also work against you if you are trying to convince a person that is skeptical about your opinion.

Make Gestures to Show That You Are Listening

Asides making eye contact, body language is another effective way of maintaining a presence. Nodding your head does this trick much more than any other gesture. Note, you have to be careful with these nods as doing it too much will come off as though you are trying too hard to impress the person you are conversing with. This will result in a decrease in your power in the eyes of the other person. Ensure you nod only when it is appropriate, and this will demand that you listen to know when it's okay to nod.

Ask Questions for Clarification

Asking questions to clarify issues or things you are not sure about is a very easy way to show someone that you were there with them as they were talking. For instance, you may ask questions like, "when you say 'hype,' you mean what?" Another way to ask clarifying questions is by paraphrasing what the person has already said. For instance, "You mean you have the recipe for the bread? Am I getting you?"

When you are in casual scenes or conversations, you can also ask questions like "what is your favorite movie?" or "What do you consider as the hardest part of being a teacher? Generally, people tend to enjoy it when they reflect on such questions and when they answer them.

Don't fidget

When you fidget, it gives the other person the impression that you are not comfortable or satisfied with the conversation and that they would rather be elsewhere. So, when you are talking to someone, be careful not to fondle your thumbs or play with something in front of you. You should also be careful not to excessively look around the place to see what else is going on around you. This will make it look as if you unsettled, and it will make the other person think you are looking out for a better chance than you already have.

Don't Focus on Finding a Response to the Person As They Are Still Talking

People tend to do this easily. In fact, almost everyone does this. Our innate selfishness is always ready to chip in response as soon as there is a chance to do so. Unfortunately, the fact that you are already thinking of what you are going to say indicates that you are not paying full attention to whatever the other person has to say. It is only natural to want to have something to say before you say it, but it is ideal for working through the response you are going to give as you are giving it. Savor every moment that you have to pause and enjoy the conversation to the fullest.

Pause for Two Seconds Before You Respond

You can break-in at the very moment the last speaker pauses or immediately after he has stopped talking. It shows that you were already thinking of what you were going to say even before he or she stopped talking, instead of paying attention to what they were saying. Non-verbal communication always seems to be more effective than verbal communication so you can make use of the following tricks to prove that you are present in the conversation:

When a person is done talking to you, first try to make use of your facial expression to show that you have assimilated what the person said to you. You can then make a striking statement to give the person's speech the consideration that it deserves. After you have done this for about two seconds, you can now give your answer.

You may consider the following sequence:

- They finish making their statements.
- You absorb their speech with your face.
- React also with your face.
- Then you can finally give your answer.

Power

Charismatic people come off as very powerful people, but it does not always mean that they hold strong leadership positions or are successful entrepreneurs. The reality is that most times, the most influential people are found in the humblest sides of life.

By the mere fact that powerful people can influence the world around them, they find it easier to get things done or give the impression that they can get things done. What charismatic people do is to attract people into their circle like a magnet. Their power is the core of this magnetic force and the primary point of attraction.

Looking back to the times when humans lived in caves, the survival of a person could be dependent on being friendly with bigwigs that were at that time, at the top of the social hierarchy.

During those times, those bigwigs had the power to give protection and give assurance for food, spouses, and general survival. To be able to get more latch into these types of people, the human brain further developed to interpret body language and other markers that can easily indicate the status of a person, as well as power.

The good thing is that humans had since moved past this era several centuries ago. However, people are still attracted to those who possess valuable resources or people who seem to know how to get those resources. Though the survival of humans may no longer depend mainly on the connection one has with such people, the possibility of one having access to higher personal and professional opportunities can depend on such connections.

Therefore, it is important to note that every one of the three components of charisma must work together if one must come to the point of magnetism. Although you may appear to be the most pleasant and the best listener in the room, if you do not have power, you are likely to be merely seen as the nice guy or worse still, seen as a desperate person This may look harsh, but the truth is that people place value on your presence and warmth according to the amount of power they think you have. Look at it this way: if you have done an excellent job and you get complimented by a co-worker and the manager of the company, which of the compliment will be valued? For most people, the compliment from the manager will be more appreciated because he is the one with more power.

On the other hand, a person who has power and is devoid of warmth and presence will not pass for a charismatic person. When a person is powerful but lacks these qualities, he will be considered as an impressive and important person, but he will appear to be aloof, nonchalant, arrogant, and cold.

Increasing your Charismatic Power

Increasing your charismatic power may seem difficult at first. It may look the same way as applying for a job that demands experience before you can be hired, but you need to secure the job before you can get the required experience. You need to keep in mind that charisma is all about the perception that other people have of you; you don't need a large amount of money or know so many influential people to be charismatic.

To gain power, you have to give the impression that you already have that power. This is mostly a 'fake it until you make it situation.' When people can perceive your supposed charismatic power, they will invite you into their circle of influence, and then, you will gain power in the real sense of it. This will equip you to practice charismatic power by building a more virtuous circle, capable of earning you more success.

Giving the impression of power boils down to boosting those things that humans naturally consider when they are trying to determine the level at which a person possesses power. This may be in terms of body language or appearance. Below are ways you can boost your charismatic power:

Enhance Your Confidence

The possession of power begins from the mind. If you are confident in the fact that you are powerful, other people will start to feel the same way about you. Being able to reassure yourself will give you an aura that cannot be easily resisted, and this will attract people to you because they will want to know more about you. Building confidence is crucial to gain power, and it is noteworthy to understand that the core of confidence lies in one's ability to master it.

A person who can gain expertise in any skill or area of knowledge will come off as one who has resources at his disposal. In the same light, he will come off as one who has enough willpower and perseverance to go into the deepest parts of a particular subject. When you can gain mastery of a specific topic, it will also boost the way you look, feel, and carry yourself.

Know A Little About So Many Topics/Things

As a plus to your self-worth, you should not only focus on your area of expertise. You should also strive to know as much as you can about different subjects. If you must be that man who can influence the world, intelligence should be one of your greatest fortes. The more you can join in conversations and add to them, the smarter you will be perceived, and the more likable you will become. To gain a wide range of knowledge, you have to keep reading and never stop learning. With every chance you get, learn something new.

Be Physically Fit

When people meet you for the first time, the shape of your body is one of the things that they take note of. A person who has a fit, muscular physique comes off as one who is strong. This type of frame sends a signal to the primary parts of the brains of others about your ability to protect and dominate. A physically fit body will also make others perceive you as one who has discipline and can endure pain to achieve a greater goal. This may be the reason why those men who are well-built seem to be wealthier than their obese and skinny counterparts.

Dress for Power

One of the most potent and earliest power cues is how a person is dressed. When you see a military man dressed in his military uniform with ribbons and stars on his shoulder, the first thing that will readily come to your mind is 'authority.' To create this impression, the military person does not have to scream it at the top of his voice or show off his stars. This also goes with the type of regular clothing you wear. While it is okay to dress modest, studies have shown that high-status dressing can influence other people.

Asides the fact that your dressing makes you appear to others as a powerful person when you dress well, your confidence will get boosted, and you will even begin to feel powerful yourself. When you feel more powerful, you do things as one who is powerful, and this will make others perceive you that way. This is known as the virtuous charismatic circle.

Act as the Big "Gorilla"

Asides clothing, there is also another feature that influences the way other people look at you in terms of power, and that is body language. This is the paralinguistic cues that show the power, and it deals mostly with the amount of space a person makes use of. As you may have already pictured in your head, powerful people usually make use of more space than those who are not. Powerful people are like 'big gorillas.'

Deborah Grunfeld, a professor in organizational behavior, describes powerful people as *"People who sit sideways on chairs, drape their arms over the back, or appropriate two chairs by placing their arm across the back of an adjacent chair. They put their feet on the desk. They sit on the desk."*

If you wish to boost the viewpoint of other people as regards the power you possess, you have to figure out ways to increase the amount of space you take up subtly. Try draping your hand across the back of your chair or sit on the desk instead of sitting behind it when a colleague comes to have a chat with you in the office.

Take on Power Poses

This is quite related to being the big gorilla. Power poses means that you are going to place your body in a way that will portray power. The most popular power pose is putting one's hand akimbo by making the hands rest on the waist. This kind of posture is very common among superheroes. You can also consider resting back on your chair and placing your hand at the back of your head. Putting your feet on the table wouldn't be a bad idea. Whichever you do, don't overdo it.

During a meeting, you can decide to portray power in the room by standing up and leaning forward. While you do this, your hands should be rested on the table before you. This will make you look like the most important person in the room at that time, and you are going to carry that air of authority with you afterward.

You can also try to lift your arms straight into the air like one who has just made a touchdown pass to decide the fate of a game. Though one cannot clearly state at what point this pose is more likely to work, it can be imbibed into your everyday life in a way that will not look too weird.

Interestingly, all of these poses will not only make you look powerful to other people, but they will also make you feel powerful. Merely assuming a power pose for a few minutes can increase your testosterone levels and reduce the level of cortisol in your body. This will increase your level of confidence and reduce your stress level. By feeling more confident, you will begin to act more powerfully. This, on its own, is another feature of the charismatic virtuous circle.

Take Charge of Your Environment

People usually have a level of self-assurance, ease, and power when they are in familiar terrain. When a person is familiar with his environment, he gains a level/sense of control, and this is what boosts his level of confidence. It is for reasons like this that many organizations will prefer to choose their location even before they begin with negotiations. Both sides of the divide typically want to feel at home, so they both want a familiar terrain.

Note, you may not always be the one to choose your environment, so you have to learn to be at home in every new location. You may ask, how is it possible to be comfortable in a room that you are entering for the first time? There are some little things which experts recommend for getting control of one's surroundings. For instance, you walk into a restaurant, try to rearrange the things on the table you are going to sit on. You may choose to move the jug or the saltshaker. This may seem like a funny idea, but when you do this, you unconsciously have an idea that you are in control of the things that are around you. This will make you feel confident and magnetic. In your everyday life, you can look out for little and polite ways of being in charge of your environment. The result of this will be amazing.

Say Few Things and Say Them Slowly

Powerful people do not only occupy physical space but also, they take up space in conversations. This is a bit of a paradox because it does not demand that you hog upon the time you have to speak. Unlike people who are not as influential, powerful people are prone to speaking fewer words. By the mere fact that they make sure that their words are scarce, powerful people add a lot of value to the words they speak. Whenever they talk, people will want to listen to them. You can try out this tip; being less of the chatty type and being more laconic with the way you talk will help you a lot.

When in conversations, powerful people fill up space with silence. Unlike most people, awkward silence isn't so awkward to powerful people. As a matter of fact, they savor those silent moments. These types of people have come to the understanding that people naturally want to fill up silent gaps, and it is the nervousness that comes with wanting to do this that they devour some strategic or useful piece of information. This is the reason why investigators, negotiator, and interviewers rely on silence to bring out the vulnerability of the other person to capitalize on it.

Talking slowly is also another way in which people consume space in conversations. People who speak fast portray a sense of anxiety and nervousness, while those who speak slowly displays a sense of thoughtfulness, intelligence, and calmness that powerful people possess. Powerful people speak slowly while the less powerful ones talk fast because if they are not fast with the things they have to say, people will not listen to them. This is the basic rule of human nature. Play a record of yourself talking, and you will be quite surprised by how fast you talk. If you make an effort to slow down, you will soon master it. Although in the beginning, it is going to seem as though you are talking too slowly, but once you can master it, you are going to sound normal and even excellent.

Improve Your Poise

One of the common traits of powerful people is composure. There is a sense of grace and stillness in them, and they have poise. Powerful people will not be caught nodding excessively as a sign of being submissive, and they will not be fidgety as a result of being nervous. Powerful people will not be found in need of verbal fillers like 'um' and 'uh,' so next time you have to interact with people, you should try to be as natural as possible while you remain focused on being still. You should nod at intervals to indicate your presence, but don't turn yourself to a lizard by nodding all the time. Make sure your hand is still and do not tap your feet excessively.

Warmth

A person who emanates warmth is generally perceived by others as one who is caring, easy-going, and empathetic because people feel comfortable being around them, and they are also at peace with them. Every human being wishes to be understood, acknowledged, and taken care of. A warm spirit takes care of all of these. It satisfies the craving of wanting to gain solid grounds in our beings from childhood to adulthood. Warmth is taking care of a person when they haven't asked to be taken care of, or caring for an individual despite having messed up. Warmth is giving a friend a shoulder to lean on or giving kudos when it is due.

Regardless of how old a person is or how independent they have become, everyone appreciates the feeling of being cared for or being at peace with someone. The same with power and presence, warmth is important to balance all the other elements as it also cannot work effectively on its own. A person who has power but is devoid of warmth will be perceived as cold and arrogant, while one who has warmth without power will be seen as a weak person who seeks validation by wanting to please everyone.

Amongst the three elements of charisma, warmth is usually the most difficult to fake. Typically, people can manage to convince others that they are present even though their minds seem to have wandered a little bit. They can also easily act like they have got their life in one piece when the reality is that they are still struggling to achieve their goals. People somehow manage to figure out when a person is faking warmth and when they figure this out, they seem to withdraw a little bit from such people because they have been made to assume that they are showing a fake version of themselves.

This element of charisma will easily backfire if those around you can figure out that the reason why you are giving it is that you wish to get something from them. This is the reason why people tend to dislike marketers who try to come off as nice because they are desperate to close a deal to secure their paycheck. This is not to say that it is bad to want something from people; if we were true to ourselves, we would all agree that the major point of charisma is the ability to influence others to do something in our favor. Regardless of whatever the case may be, whether you are trying to have them buy a particular good or services, or go on a date with you, the point is that you shouldn't seek to influence people solely for your selfish gains.

If warmth must be genuine, it has to be based on something that goes beyond selfish reasons. It must be as a result of one's satisfaction with life and as a result of empathy and curiosity about others. A person who has genuine warmth will not hesitate to know people from different works of life. This type of person has the mindset that despite they are not able to get what they need from their interaction with the other person, they will still be grateful to have met the person because they feel their interaction with such people is worth their time and effort.

If warmth must be effective in creating an endearing spirit, the outward attitudes that show a sense of warmth to other people must come from a powerful, yet the indescribable quality that comes from a genuine heart. The root of charismatic warmth begins from the crux of an individual.

Creating Warmth from Within

There are some people that being with them is intoxicating. These people have a way of making you feel important and notice. At the end of a conversation with such people, they will linger in your thoughts; you don't necessarily have to be in a romantic relationship with them to feel this way. These people have warmth from within, which they give to make you have these feelings.

People that create warmth from within have the power to captivate your attention. They make you notice them when they speak, make you listen to them, and make you open to their influence. Spending a little time with them will always make your mood brighter. People with warmth are always enjoyed, sought-after, trusted, and influential and remembered. This magic of creating warmth doesn't lie in what they say or how they make you feel it lies in two practices, and anyone can learn it.

If you wish to create warmth from within yourself, there are two ways to go about it:

Show Gratitude

A heart that is full of gratitude is a happy one. Research has shown that those who show gratitude every day are happy people. People who show gratitude are more positive than those who do not show gratitude.

To create a grateful heart, you can choose to write those things that you are truly grateful for. Every day of your life, once you can portray a spirit of gratitude, you will be able to put the things that bother you into perspective. This will help you to stay relaxed by having a spirit of contentment which reflects in your interaction with others and will also put them at ease when they are with you.

Be Empathetic

Empathy can be said to be a "fellow feeling." This is the most important feature that can help one to live a healthy social and political life. If you must develop charismatic warmth, this is a crucial factor to consider. Generally, people appreciate being understood, and it is empathy that helps us to put ourselves in other people's shoes to feel the way they are feeling.

Certainly, it is not easy to develop empathy because there are a lot of things to discourage it in modern times, and these things can make you cynical about the state of humans. Regardless, it is possible to develop it. Here are some tips that will help you to reduce this cynicism and gain more empathy for other people:

See Others as Your Brothers and Sisters

This is a mindset that has roots in religious beliefs which holds that all humans were created by the same God, or in the scientific theory that believes humans have their origin from a certain place in the African continent. This scientific belief also holds that everyone is made of the same stardust.

Whether religious or scientific, one thing that is arguably certain is that all humans are cosmically connected. This may sound cheesy, but the thought that everyone is family members that are journeying through the same path will help you to show more compassion to others even at times when you need to feel otherwise.

Interact with Others Physically

Studies have shown that college students had become less empathetic than their counterparts over the years. What could be the reason for this decline? The answer to this may be in the fact that people now interact less physically as humans now operate as disembodied individuals on the internet. There is a lot of power in physical interactions; the mere sight of people's facial expressions is enough to trigger a feeling of empathy in people.

When these physical cues are not available, it becomes possible to portray evil motives towards other people as these motives can easily go unchecked/unpunished. You may want to consider stepping away from your keyboard often and step into the real world to interact with people. If you can do this, you will gain another perspective of humans asides the terrible viewpoint you had of them as a result of your interactions online.

Think of a Different Story about Those That Annoy You

As you are rushing to meet up with your interview, the chances are that you, at one point, had to cut someone off while you were driving. Though you hate to have done that, you tell yourself that it is something you had to do to secure the job. When the tables are turned, and you are the one that was being cut off, you judge the person who had done that to be wicked. This is because it is easy to make excuses for our misdemeanors because we think they are things we had to do, while we consider the same attitudes from others as a flaw in their character. This does not have to be so. You can try to be a bit more compassionate about others the same way you are to yourself, by imagining the reasons why they possibly acted rudely or were so annoying to you.

Be Curious About Others

If you must put yourself in other people's shoes, you must first try to know them. This is the reason why you have to ask questions for clarification to see things from their points of view and also, to be able to know the reason why they have become how they are. With every meeting comes the possibility of getting to know about the human experience. Do not miss any chance.

The more you can develop empathy, the more you find out that every human is going through one hard stuff or the other. When you can realize the fact that there is a struggle for every man, you will feel the need to be a source of relieve for others. You will naturally want to be that person who lightens the burdens of others by making them feel understood, safe, and tranquilized even within the shortest time.

Showing Warmth to Others

Since one cannot easily fake warmth because it is something a person must nurture from within, let's consider the roles of our outward attributes to this element of charisma.

First, we have to ask ourselves if it is possible for a person to have a good heart but not good at showing kindness to other people. Sometimes, people are aware of the fact that they are too careless about emotions, although they will like to think that they are good people. The truth is that having inner warmth alone isn't enough. One's ability to show this warmth to those around them also matters a lot.

Also, the level of warmth a person shows on the outside influences the warmth he feels on the inside. This is a virtuous circle. The more warmth you show to others, the more warmth you feel inside, and this is what makes you warm towards others. As a matter of fact, if you can show warmth, you will also be developing your inner warmth at a quick pace and even more effectively. You don't have to wait to feel like you are an empathetic person before you start acting like one. Naturally, you become what you act as. So, you should make efforts to work on your behavior and your mindset simultaneously. They both work hand in hand.

You don't have to worry yourself with thoughts of appearing fake as a result of acting warmly before you actually feel it inside. What matters most is the fact that you have a good motive for your actions.

Below, I will be discussing some behaviors that you can easily pull off if you are not awkward about them, and if you are not doing them exaggeratedly. They are easy ways in which you can put your best foot forward with people you interact with. If you are trying it for the first time, you may feel a bit awkward about it, but you don't have to worry because you have to begin somewhere. Once you start practicing them, the charismatic warmth circle will begin, and with time, it will register as an entirely genuine act.

Consider Yourself as a Host

Imagine a scenario when you have people visiting you at home. What are those things that you do naturally as a host? Certainly, the most important thing to you is such cases is the comfort of your guests. Now try to imbibe this mindset in your interactions with others. Whenever you are thinking of yourself as a host, you would easily figure out what you can do to make other people at ease.

Give Sincere Compliments

Nothing works better than a sincere compliment in tensed situations. It is capable of strengthening relationships and melting hearts. It is too bad that people tend to be very stingy with kind words. It may not be your style, but you have to learn how to give compliments as it will make a lot of things easier. You can also learn ways of accepting compliments also.

Your Voice Should Reflect More Warmth

Naturally, our voice carries a lot of emotions, and it is not only reflected in the way we say things, but it also reflects in the tone with which we say them, as well as the pitch we use. When we are angry, we tend to speak in loud and harsh tones, while kindness and warmth are reflected in softer and milder tones to imbibe warmth in your tone. Instead, you can take the easy route of smiling when you are talking.

This communicates a sense of instant warmth. This will be a lot helpful in non-physical communications like when you are talking on the phone. Though you do not have body language and facial expressions at your disposal in such situations, you can use your voice, which at that point is your only tool to communicate warmth.

Offer Your "Kind Eyes"

Some people have what can be described as kind eyes. This kind of look is reflected in the gaze that people give, which makes others at peace, understood, and accepted. However, it is possible for someone to have this kind of eyes, yet not be a good person; these are the kind of people that can switch from being nice from afar to being a beast when you get closer to them. Although your world may be crumbling right in front of them, they will give you a look that will make you feel like everything is alright, while they could have actually helped you to save the situation.

A person's eyes are the pathway to his soul, and when you have kind eyes, it reflects the goodness of your heart. However, there are ways in which a person can boost the kindness that is reflected in his eyes in order for it to truly depict his inner warmth. To have a kind heart, you can switch your look to a milder focus. Instead of giving a squint or a stare like you are about to punch the person that is in front of you, you can actually relax your gaze and broaden your focus. When you are able to feel like your face is relaxed around your eyes, you are most likely to have been able to achieve 'kind eyes.'

Anticipate Needs

You may always choose to give something to people without them asking for it. This shows that you care about them, and you are looking out for them. For example, you may choose to get your colleague at work a cup of coffee because you feel it is going to help them. Think about offering your jacket to someone because you think they might need it on a cold winter morning or simply giving someone a hand.

Offer a Warm Drink

A warm drink has a magical feel that gives people warm feelings, so you see, offering a cup of coffee might have a bit of a psychological impact on the person you gave it to as it will also generate a feeling of warmth towards you. Well, this may be the reason why coffee shops are a top choice for business meetings and first dates.

Give a Firm/Good Handshake

One of the best ways to influence warmth in another person is by touch. Though you may have to/want to respect people's space and not touch them in ways that may be considered inappropriate (especially in a flirty manner). Because there are rules, a handshake may be the most appropriate way to make skin-to-skin contact, so you may want to make good use of it with every opportunity you get.

If you wish to give your handshake a boost that will induce warmth, you can extend your index finger to the inner part of the wrist of the other person while you are clasping your hands. According to some experts in communication, when you touch the pulse point of a person while you are shaking hands with them, they will feel a sense of connection towards you.

Try to Know the Effort That Other People Are Putting into Things

There is some sort of little martyr in everyone, and we all want people to take note of the trouble that we faced to get something done. While we all have these cravings, it may be a little awkward to list them out. The best way to go about acknowledging the efforts of others is by having them tell you about it by asking questions that will give them the chance to talk about it. If, for example, a friend has driven long hours to see you, you can ask about the things he had to pass through or those he had to forfeit to see you.

Make Them Feel at Ease

People will always be grateful for those that help them avoid the feeling of being alone. You can easily show warmth by introducing people to your circle and having them join in on your conversations or ideas. You should also learn how to be able to master the art of taking charge of conversations by learning how to engage in small talks effectively. People always like to have someone at a particular gathering whom they are sure will be able to keep the conversation running.

Remember Details like Dates and Anniversaries

Everyone likes the feeling that comes with someone else remembering their birthdays. This will go a long way to help someone feel loved and important. This does not have to do with merely sending texts or posting birthday messages on the person's Facebook wall. Going extra miles to send cards or sending emails will count for so much more. This will not only be an avenue to wish them happy birthdays, but it will also be an opportunity to catch up with their welfare. This also goes for other milestones and anniversaries.

It is also possible to show warmth by remembering other details like the name of a person and that of their loved ones. Asking after the welfare of the people they care about will mean a lot to them as well.

Give Thoughtful Gifts

This is not talking about gift cards, and it does not also have to be big gifts. Thoughtful gifts are simply those gifts that will show that you paid attention to the needs of another person. When a person you care about mentions what he likes and what he is interested in having, you can simply lock the idea away in your head, or you can even make a note about it. They will definitely be happy if, at a later time, you come up with that same thing they have mentioned that they would like to have.

Also, these gifts may be something they make a habit of acquiring, say a pack of the person's favorite drink. It would make the person happy to have you show up unexpectedly with something he/she truly likes.

Sort Things Out

If someone is facing a problem and you can help them take care of it, do so without hesitation. If, for example, they have a question that you do not have an answer to, you can simply say you don't know, but you will help them find out. If there is a task that you can assist them in, give them a hand. You know there is a deadline to meet, so you have offered to help. This will mean a whole lot to the person.

Remember that you do not have to be a pushover to convey warmth, but if there is any way you can help a friend with your time or expertise, do so. You can always do your best to do something that will, at least, lighten someone else's burden.

Be Liberal with Appreciations

It is possible to show warmth without being physically present. A simple thank you note is one of the best ways to do this. There is no single time that can be considered a bad time to show appreciation. A simple thank you note will make people realize that you noticed their effort, and you took out time to acknowledge the fact that they have done something or to acknowledge their place in your life. You may possibly pen this down by hand and put it in an envelope. The receiver will certainly smile when they receive it.

Chapter 3: Ways of Improving your Charisma

There are some people that seem to be naturally likable - it always looks like they were born likable. Well, this may be true, but you can also train yourself to become likable. No matter what your personality type is, you can always train yourself to exhibit some traits through constant practice. You can apply these traits to your character so that you can become more attractive, influential, and even trustworthy. Below are some basic tips for developing your charisma.

Start from Wearing a Warm Smile

A warm smile can never go wrong; it is a good point to start. With a smile, you will be able to set an emotional tone that will carry the audience with you on a journey. As you are speaking, you hope to get certain reactions of joy, suspense, anxiety, pride, concern, hope, or fear. You should be able to win all of these from your audience while you still appear to your audience like the Mr. Nice Guy.

Create an Emotional Connection with Your Audience When You Speak

Speaking is one of the earliest practices of humans. The earliest records of speech can be traced back to about fifty to a hundred thousand years ago. The oral tradition has made a lot of impacts on humans as it has molded all the societies of the earth over the years. This is certainly a lot of years for humans to be able to use this phenomenon to perfect their influence on other people and also situations.

Over the ages, there's been a lot of examples that one can reckon with when it comes to influential speaking. Abraham Lincoln, Winston Churchill, Martin Luther King, and the likes are some of these examples. These people were able to capture the attention of their audiences with every word that they spoke. What they had, which is the thing that made them stand out among their equals, was a very important life skill—charisma. When they spoke, it didn't matter who they were talking to or the number of their audience, they spoke in a way that their speech was felt by the members of the audience as though they were addressing each individual personally.

They all had styles that made them appear as though they didn't have to put in so much effort to deliver their thoughts in a well-fashioned manner. This is the technique that they used to captivate their audience.

Every time they moved as they spoke, their movements were in tune with the words they spoke, and they had an appearance that suited/appealed to the senses of their audience.

In line with the three elements of charisma, with effective practice and a lot of self-confidence, everyone will be able to gain charisma with this tip.

Also, what matters is the perception you have of your audience. The number of times that you have practiced before a mirror does not really matter; neither does the opinion of those around you about your message matters. Even though you may have an excellent speech to deliver, if you do not create an emotional connection with your audience, your message will not mean so much to your audience.

Typically, when people sit to listen to you, they do so with hopes that they are going to learn something new, so they listen with a sense of sympathy. What they want is to be inspired or to have a glimpse of your journey, so you have to make sure that you can give them what they want. What makes it easy is that they are open to bonding with you and building a relationship with you. This means that from the moment you start speaking, you have to set your mind at connecting with them.

Perfect the Mechanics of Speech

To be considered as one who speaks well, you have to space your words and your ideas. To do this, you have to be expressive with the tone which you deliver your speech with, and this should be at the right moments too. Try to breathe well and have enough energy to deliver your speech.

Make room for your listeners to pause when they should. This is very important for any speech. The best orators can space their speech in a way that allows the audience to be able to digest their ideas as they consider the next thing they are going to say. It is only very few people that can combine speaking and thinking. The power of your speech and what enables it to make the desired impact lies with the silences that come in the middle of your speech.

Tone also matters a lot in speech as it has some subtle effects that you may not easily take note of. If you are able to adopt the right tone and you can control your voice by chipping in the necessary emotional hints when they are appropriate, you will be able to control and make sure of the fact that your audience does not have doubts about the message you wish to pass across. When you maintain the right body language, your speech will naturally find the right tone.

As you talk, you are going to need a good amount of air to help you pass your message across. Can you recall the number of times you have witnessed people going off track on their speech when what they actually need to be doing is to be placing more emphasis on the theme of their message? It is very common for speakers to end their speech with the most important parts of their messages.

Ensure that you take in a good amount of air into your diaphragm such that you get the required energy that will help you deliver your last line with a 'blast.'

Your Body Should Match Your Words

Your audience will naturally feel uncomfortable if they notice that there is a disconnection between the things you are saying and the way you are saying them. When you are giving a positive message, for an instant, your body language should not in any way be defensive because it will arouse the suspicions of your audience as to whether you are being. Also, a positive message with a static body will also make the audience to feel you are not as excited about your message as you would want them to believe.

As you are speaking, you have to move at every point the language you use demands that you move. Make use of gestures and demonstrations when necessary to emphasize your words rather than trying to get attention from it. Make use of facial expressions to give you hints about the way they are supposed to feel. With this, they will be able to flow with you at the same level.

Your Message Should Be Compelling

When you tell personal, authentic, and valid stories, your audience will be able to relate with you. This will bring you closer to them because, to them, you are no longer a distant voice from the podium. You may even become as close to them as a voice in their head or as a part of them, which they can always turn to; you become one that is sitting right next to them, who is sharing a special part of his/her journey with them.

There is a very special feeling that comes with a person confiding in another, and everyone can relate to that feeling. If an audience of different people and personalities are able to connect with you peculiarly, you would have won the crowd to yourself.

As you speak, your message has to assume a logical structure that is centered on a particular theme. It should be woven around a foundation that you are going to build upon as you proceed in the course of your speech. Your speech is best from a credible place that your audience is going to accept because they believe what you are saying. You must ensure that you don't make the deadly mistake of making your audience feel judged. Certainly, no one wants to face judgment day so early.

Practice Mirroring

If you wish to be charismatic at the moment, try to mirror your qualities. This entails that you try to adopt the qualities of someone else (someone you admire or whom you consider to be a charismatic person). Try to match up with his gestures, mannerisms, and his energy. By doing this, you are going to notice that people will respond to the attributed you have mirrored just as they would with the person whose attributes you are adopting. This does not mean that you are going to agree with all the things they do or everything they say. The only thing you are imitating to a reasonable extent, the way they act. This may come quite naturally for you, but it depends largely on your social setting. However, it is a simple way of boosting your likeability.

In doing this, you have to select those qualities that you consider to be likable to other people. Observation is a very important factor in your journey to improving your charisma. As Joyce Newman, the head of the Newman Group, says, you have to look up to those people whom you consider as charismatic. According to him, you don't have to imitate them; what you need to do is to learn their secrets, then apply them to yourself. You should polish them until they suit you perfectly. Note that this is a process of trial and error.

Take Hollywood or any other industry, for example, and you will notice that there are charismatic people everywhere. Note the way the best actors in these industries carry themselves. Use them as your yardstick by picking their most effective and charismatic qualities for your use. By emulating those people whom you think are likable, you will be able to learn some things about how you can also become likable.

Have Fun

People make the mistake of associating public speaking with a feeling of horror, inconvenience, freight, anxiety, or even torture as if the entire process or experience is a scene from a nightmare. It does not have to be like this when you speak (to a large or small audience), you should do it as though you are also a member of the audience. Think of the things you like to see in your speaker; do you want them to carry on in a stiff manner, or you prefer to see them enjoying his or her experience? I guess a lively speaker will appeal more to you.

By enjoying your presentation or speech, you give the impression that you were not forced to do what you are doing because you like that you are doing it, and not that you are doing a lot of hard work and are passing through a lot of stress.

Your audience will not only see you as one who has something important to say, but they will be grateful for the fact that they did not miss the chance to listen to you. The mere fact that you enjoy talking to them will make them feel like you have something 'cool' to give them, and it is just a matter of time before they too will begin to enjoy themselves.

Put a Lot of Energy in Your Voice

When you talk, you should be as audible as possible. Have you ever listened to someone whom you strained your ears to hear? Soft-talkers and presenters who lack energy are the types that stress their audience by making them strain their ears to listen to them. These speakers seem so far away from their audience as they make them (the audience) feel like they are being left out of the message they are meant to get.

When you speak, you should ensure that it is able to gather a lot of vocal power to enable you to get to everyone that is listening to you. This should include those that are seated at the back who would ordinarily not find it easy to hear you. Keep in mind that your vocal energy varies in different scenarios as it will need to be high with a large audience and in an open space. When you are using a mic, also, you should ensure that you tone your voice down. If you notice that where you are speaking in is echoing, you should try to speak slowly so that you will not end up overriding your speech.

By projecting the necessary amount of energy during a presentation, everything will be made easy for those who are listening to you. They will feel relaxed instead of stressing to help you do a part of your job.

Chapter 4: Improving Your Self-Confidence

In everything you do, and in almost every part of your life, confidence is very important, but not everybody has this life skill as a vast majority of people find themselves struggling with it. This can be a very tedious, vicious circle, and it makes it very difficult for people who are not confident to be able to record success in their lives.

It is not everyone that is lucky to be born with an innate sense of self-confidence, and sometimes, it proves very difficult for people to learn this attribute. This may either be a result of some personal experiences or as a result of low self-esteem. All of these are the reasons why people struggle with themselves.

Here are some attributes of a confident person:

- They do the things they believe in, even though people may consider it to be awkward.
- A confident person is not afraid of taking risks.
- Accepts their mistakes and learns from them
- They can take compliments
- Confident people are optimists.

Generally, people are not willing to accept or back projects that are pitched by a person who is nervous, fidgety and too apologetic, but a person who is able to speak clearly and defend his pitch will be able to persuade a client by holding his head high and answering questions with confidence. Admitting not to know a thing when you really don't know it also shows a high sense of confidence.

According to an online review, when a client requests for a refund or a rejection from investors can make one's self-confidence to reduce. People who pass unkind comments, albeit well-meaning to people who are close to them, also contributes to low self-confidence.

Ultimately, everyone should try to deal with the innate critic that makes room for self-doubt and constantly tells them that they are not good enough when you are faced with those things that pose a threat to your confidence. People should be able to build up their self-confidence by themselves regardless of what is happening around them.

If you must be successful in your business or anything you venture into in life, you have to develop a thick skin and a confidence level that cannot be shaken. This will help you to conquer all the obstacles that will come your way.

Below are some helpful tips that can help you boost your self-confidence:

Create a Mental Picture of Who You Want to Be

You can achieve anything you set your mind to as long as you believe it. With visualization, which is a method that entails that you create an image of yourself becoming that person that you will be proud of, you will do almost everything with an assurance that you are going to succeed. People who struggle with low self-esteem usually have a perception of themselves that is not true.

If you want to boost your confidence, you should picture that exceptional image of yourself and work towards achieving it.

Be Affirmative

Affirmations are tools that are used to imbibe favorable beliefs about one's self. Generally, people behave according to the ways they picture themselves. The first thing to do in making effective, long-lasting changes is to change the way you see yourself.

An affirmation is a positive statement that we say to ourselves to uplift our spirit. Most times, they tend to be more efficacious when they are said audibly in a way that we can hear. You will easily believe whatever you say to yourself often. If, for example, you do not like the way you look, you can practice reminding yourself of those things that you like or appreciate about yourself every time you look into the mirror.

For you to allow yourself accept and believe those positive statements quickly, your affirmations should be stated as a question like, "why do I have such beautiful dentition?" instead of merely saying that you have a beautiful dentition. The human brain is fond of trying to get answers to questions even when those questions are not valid.

Do Something That Scares You Daily

If you feel insecure, the chances are that the whole world is also insecure, so don't exaggerate your competition and don't also underestimate yourself. You are always better than you think you are. One of the best things to do when you are trying to overcome fears is to face it squarely. If you do something that you are afraid of every day, you will gain a lot of confidence from experience, and with time, your self-confidence will be significantly increased. You have to step out of your comfort zone and confront your fears.

Challenge Your Inner Critic

Since you have, for so many years, criticized yourself, try something different by approving yourself and see whether it is going to work. Most times, the harshest comments come from the voice in our heads, which is the voice of our inner critic. If you notice that you are struggling with low self-esteem, the chances are that there is an inner critic that has become too active and inaccurate.

You can adopt techniques like Cognitive Behavioral Therapy to help you challenge this inner critic. It will help you to seek evidence that either supports or denies the things that your inner critic is telling you. If, for example, you feel like you are a never-do-well, seek evidence to prove or deny this thought.

You should also look for every chance to congratulate, reward, or compliment yourself for the smallest of successes that you record. According to Mark Twain, a person can never be comfortable without getting approval from himself.

Set Yourself Up for Success

To gain true self-confidence, a person has to set his mind on his own successes and neglect his failures as well as other negative aspects of his life. Most times, people get discourages about their own strengths because they set goals that they cannot achieve for themselves. You should begin by setting small, achievable goals for yourself. By first creating a line of successes that you can quickly achieve, you will be able to proceed to more challenging goals. You should ensure that you have a list of the things you have achieved, including the big and the small ones. This will remind you of the fact that you have done well several times.

Instead of spending a lot of time brooding over the things you have to do, you might consider thinking about the ones you have accomplished. By reflecting on your milestones, the projects you have completed, and the goals you have achieved, you will be able to reassure yourself about your skills.

Lend a Helping Hand to Someone

By giving a hand to someone else, people tend to forget about their selves and feel grateful for the things they have. There is also a very good feeling that is associated with being a part of someone else's success or helping someone to make a difference.

Rather than focusing on your weaknesses, you should offer to mentor, teach, or assist someone else. By doing this, you will notice that your confidence in yourself has improved as a result of helping someone else grow.

Take Care of Yourself

You are never selfish for wanting to take care of yourself. Typically, self-confidence is birthed by good physical, social, and emotional health. A person who hates his physique will not easily feel good about himself and will not be able to exhibit high energy.

Everyone should create time to work out, eat, and sleep well. Also, people should learn to dress the way they want to feel. People usually say "clothes make the man," and this is very true. Your clothes are the first introduction your make about yourself, and it goes a long way to form people's first impression of you. You should make efforts to look after the things you need for your wellbeing.

Create Personal Boundaries

You should never allow yourself to be bullied into silence, made a victim by anyone, because no one's definition of you is true. You alone have the power to define yourself.

The word 'No' shouldn't be too hard for you to say. Make others understand that you have personal boundaries, and they have to respect it. When you can, take classes on how you can be firm with your beliefs, and demand what you want and what you think you deserve from people. When you have control over your own life, you will become more confident in yourself.

Develop an Equality Mentality

You will render your real self-useless of you always wish to be someone else. Trying to be someone else is a result of low self-esteem, as it is those who have low self-esteem that considers others to be better or more worthy than they are. You do not have to carry this perception of yourself. You should rather see yourself as an equal being to everyone else because no one is better or more deserving than you are. You should create a mentality that will help you to see everyone as equal. This type of mindset is a potent tool in helping you to improve on yourself confidence- "after all, those that are doing it are not better than me, which means I can do it too."

Give Yourself Some Positive Pep Talks

Maybe you are not a motivational speaker that's going in front of an audience or even an athlete that's about going for Olympic competition, so why do you need a pep talk? Well, pep talk always works to improve your self-confidence. When we about to do something of great significance in life, we may be faced with feelings of regrets be dreadful about what we want to do. Do you find yourself saying you couldn't achieve all that you have planned for last year, why would now be any different? Or maybe you feel you are not up for the task before you. Well, if you have such thoughts, now is the best time to give yourself pep talks.

Pep talk is a short speech that you give yourself to help you feel more productive, courageous, and enthusiastic. The best pep talk can only be given to ourselves because we know what is going through our minds. We also know our strengths and weaknesses better than anybody.

You will never be confident in yourself if you are always running negative lines in your head by telling yourself how you are not good enough. Ponder on your pep talks and think about how they might have affected your confidence level. Think about the way you will typically treat your best friend and become your own biggest cheerleader.

Find Your Hobby

Finding a hobby you love goes a long way in boosting your self-confidence. It can lower your stress and give you an overall increased sense of purpose and belonging. Hobbies can have a quality impact on your life. When you have something (meaningful hobbies) you engaged in outside your work life, you have this happiness and self-confidence that spills over. It gives you focus and more enthusiastic about the things you do.

Discover those things or something you like doing and are very passionate about. This could be singing, photography, hiking, drawing, or anything at all. When you have discovered the things that you can never get tired of doing, you should become determined to try it out and make a habit of doing it. Generally, when people are interested or passionate about something, they are likely always to feel motivated to engage in them; hence, their skills in that thing will improve significantly. Most times, when people do things they are not passionate about, they tend to fail in them, and this is one of the causes of low self-esteem.

Chapter 5: Speaking with Charisma; Tips on Improving your Public Speaking Skills

Most times, public speakers fall into the tip of desperation from the need to demonstrate to their audience that they have that flame of confidence that will thrill their audience. However, gaining charisma in public actually goes beyond wanting to be charismatic. Though it is a learnable skill, it demands a lot of hard work. It is a valuable and magical aura that a person either has or doesn't have- it has no middle ground.

Practicing Charisma in Public Speaking

Just like in many other ventures in life, exhibiting charisma in public speaking is something every passionate public speaker can learn. It is just like the way you feel when you are comfortable with your skin. There are cases where people are not happy with their skins, but certainly, they can learn to embrace and carry their selves with confidence. This is the same with charisma. Here are ways which a person can learn and practice charisma in the art of speaking:

Charisma Is Dominant in Your Comfort Zone

If you think your public speaking charisma is locked out somewhere and you are wondering where it might be, you should reach out to those places where you find yourself at ease the most. As yourself, how do you usually act when you feel comfortable? Typically, everyone has that point where they find themselves to be at peace the most. This may be in the midst of certain people whom we feel we 'flow' with the most. With these people, or at these points, we find that everything becomes much easier, and even the words come out just right. Here, there is a lot of joy and laughter, and we are most acknowledged by those around us because they are interested in the things that we have to say. These are the points where it is easier for us to access our inner charisma.

With everyone, there are some situations when we have charisma. The best way to reach out to this charisma that reflects in our favorite points to public speaking is to let it out as though we are at that favorite point again. Reflect on the places in your life where your charisma pops up and think of the things you have to do to get yourself to that point. Once you have been able to figure this out, you can simply bring it into your public speaking game.

The most important factors in public speaking charisma are:

- Feeling relaxed
- Taking charge of the situation
- Making room for your unique traits to manifest

Find Your Peculiar Charisma Spice

Some people have a wrong perception of charisma equaling, but that is a thing that is not very authentic. This perception is born out of a fixed mindset of what charisma is. When one thinks of charisma, the first things that will likely come to mind are confidence, power, a bright smile, a sleek personality, or a funny person.

In public speaking, charisma is not something you wear on your face. Even though you try to wear the look, if it isn't your style, it may not efficiently work for you. While others may manifest charisma by smiling and being funny, yours maybe is being intellectual, polished, bright, and unusual or something entirely different from what people are used to. All you have to do is to find which charisma spice is yours. What works for you may not work for me, and vice versa.

Create A Charismatic Caricature and Play with It

Once you have been able to figure out the way you are when you are at your best, you can then summon that part of you to your public speaking life.

The best way to do this is to make a charismatic caricature of yourself by overanalyzing that natural charisma of yours in a manner that may seem too big. When you do this, though, you should be careful to maintain your originality. This caricature is you, but an exaggerated version of you.

When you picture yourself standing on a stage before an audience, note that you are representing your qualities in front of your audience. With your unique attributes and characteristics, people will be able to relate to what you are made of, and this will help you to become a complete version of yourself. It will also help you to reflect on yourself within your naturally vibrant self. The audience will, in turn, be able to remember you, and your message will also become unforgettable to them. Therefore you should push yourself a little bit harder for you to become a more charismatic speaker.

Figure out Your Charismatic Attributes

Charismatic speakers are never scared of adopting new styles as long as their audience will be able to identify with the style. You have to remember that people like to know what they are going to meet when they are listening to a speaker, so it is okay to have a unique style.

Think about those things that your audience are always sure to encounter when they hear you speak;

- Is it your nice, serious nature that helps you to ensure that you always tell the truth?
- Are you the lively speaker who is always full of life?
- Are you that speaker that comes up with videos for every speech?
- Are you a vulnerable speaker that is easily penetrable while speaking?
- Is it the fact that you always involve the audience in your speech?

Whatever your unique quality is, you gave to stick with it and give your audience one thing that they can always rely on. This will make them see you as one who has charisma.

When it's all said and done, public speaking charisma is all about your confidence, so you have to do everything you can to reinforce every bit of positivity in you about yourself and stay away from negative feelings that will form a wall between you and your audience. Remember that negative self-talk forms a big barrier between you and charismatic public speaking. Therefore, challenge that inner demon that holds you back, and have a conversation with your charisma and its best friend, charisma.

When you step into the room, be yourself, and make sure you exude charisma in every way possible.

Be Authentic

Charisma is not something that can be faked. It is an attribute that comes from within, a genuine and positive motivation. It is an important set of beliefs that influence/drives a person's actions. If you are not authentic, every effort you make at being charismatic will be in futility. As a charismatic person, you need to be grounded in core ethical foundations. Generally, charismatic people are empaths who put the needs of other people first, and they push to breed positive relationships with others. They also look out for positive results from all the efforts they put in; therefore, to be charismatic, you have to be truly passionate about others.

Gain Emotional Intelligence

Emotional intelligence is a person's ability to understand and keep track of his own emotions as well as that of other people. This understanding is used to keep track of their character. A person who can develop emotional intelligence manifests this by an awareness of his self, can tame or regulate himself, and also builds quality social skills. An emotionally intelligent person is empathetic and has an innate ability to motivate and push himself. These qualities are inexhaustible qualities of a leader or a good public speaker, and a charismatic person is expected to have emotional intelligence.

Be Focused

Remember that a good public speaker requires presence, but it might be quite difficult to achieve. Typically, a millennial has a ton of work to do, and life also comes hard at people. This is usually very overwhelming and reduces a person's focus and presence. Focus for a charismatic person means that he has to shut his ears away from distractions and pay attention to the needs of his audience and everyone around. It is with a focus that a speaker can notice when he is beginning to bore his listeners; hence, he needs to shake things up a little bit. It is with a focus that a person sees opportunities, solves problems, and take things one step at a time.

Project Leadership Presence

One cannot deny the fact that our appearance, the way we speak, the way we dress, and our drive, is the way we will be addressed. When you speak, ensure that you have a relaxed body language. Being uptight will indicate tension, so you have also to be upright. Do not also forget to smile. When you speak, make sure that you use the dynamic power of your voice to impose your presence. This is where you bring in diaphragmatic breathing. Avoid filter words or jargon and also practice slow and clear speaking. If you want to be seen as a leader while you speak, so you have to act the part if you wish to be accepted as a leader. Depending on what is acceptable in your industry, you have to dress according to the ways that are socially acceptable for an ideal leader.

Keep Practicing

Ask an Olympic athlete if they only showed up for the Olympics and were asked to compete. You will definitely get a 'no' for an answer. Typically, an Olympian spends many hours to perfect their skills before they show up to compete on the D-day, and it is this practice that brings the athletes to their level of performance at every level. If this is the case, you have to ask why people think that they can escape investing in getting quality, new skills? All of the tips that have been mentioned in this section are worth practicing, so you have to practice them constantly, and they will earn you success. As a result, you will become more charismatic in speaking, as well as leadership.

Qualities of a Charismatic Speaker

Public speaking for most people can be terrifying as most people tend to freak out at the mere thought of it, but if you have a deep concern for the growth of your career, you will need to focus on ensuring that your voice is heard and public speaking is the best way you can do so. It entails you sharing your thoughts and ideas with a good number of people and keep your head high, even amid a crowd of professionals to stay visible and relevant in your industry. Although you may have the drive and all the right motivations to get it right with public speaking, if you do not have the proper skills for it, the chances are that no one will pay attention to what you have to say so they are not going to receive the message you wish to pass across.

Here are some qualities you need to possess as a public speaker:

Confidence

Confident speakers always have the following: competence, credibility, intelligence, knowledge, likeability, and believability. These are the qualities that make the speaker more believable to his audience than those who are not as confident.

In the art of public speaking, confidence is a very important factor, although it is not the only important thing to public speaking. In the words of Mark Twain, two types of speakers exist in the world, and they are the nervous ones and the liars. When you appear before a crowd to give a speech, it is very natural for a person to be nervous, but you can overcome anxiety with either excitement or authenticity;

Excitement: If you are excited about the speech you are going to deliver, the feeling you get will help you stay above any form of nervousness that may exist during your presentation. According to studies, those who choose to take their nervousness as a feeling of excitement will be more comfortable when they speak.

Authenticity: You have to be your real self when you appear before an audience, even if it means that you have to stray from the presentation you have prepared. Though you need to practice your speech as much as you can constantly, you have to be very careful not to memorize what you have practiced because memorizing it can make you fumble in some parts of it if you in any way feel like you did not say something right. If you wish to excel in public speaking, you have to try to do more than just getting over the feeling of nervousness. You also have to be very confident in what you are going to tell your audience and also be yourself when you are on stage.

Passion

If you must pass a message to your audience during your speech, you need to be very passionate about your subject. If you are not passionate, your presentation is not going to have any meaning. As you speak to your audience, you have to reflect a high level of sincerity in your emotions. This is the only way your presentation is going to get to them and move them.

Practicing sincerity while you are practicing your speech is going to be unnecessary, even if you try to make use of gestures like a raised tone or a raised hand. All you need to do is to set your mind on the way you feel about yourself and those you are talking to.

During presentations at the workplace, it may be a little difficult to show passion about your topic, especially when you are not engaged in the activity that you have to present on. At times, if you must show passion about the topic you have to present on even though you are not passionate about it, you can do some research on the topic to see if it is possible to get things that interest you on the topic.

Authenticity

When you are on stage, you should not try to be another person because your real self will always win. Though you may have come prepared and well-rehearsed, believing in or mastering your message is sometimes not all that matters if you are not able to act like yourself when you are in front of your audience. It is the lack of authenticity that makes an audience perceive you as someone who is not sincere. It will also make it look like your speech is a well-calculated one that is made to sway their opinions to help you get to your desired end.

As a candidate of a political party, you have to appear authentic because anything less will make you lose your chance of winning the election. As a company, if you have a social media marketing strategy that does not seem authentic, you will not get enough returns on investment as you will record less engagement on your ads, and this means that your sales will not go up. A dating website or page will also not record a lot of success if you don't come up with authentic content because those that are reading what you have written will easily spot the inauthenticity in your writings. The same goes for speaking.

It is not surprising that most of the articles you find with the word 'authenticity' written on its headlines seem to have gained more attention dramatically. Authenticity is an essential factor in public speaking, and each speaker needs to look out for the best strategies that will help him/her become authentic.

Practicing, Not Memorizing

If you wish to be yourself during a presentation, you should avoid memorizing your speech. Instead, you should practice your speech as often as you can and make use of appropriate synonyms. This will make it easier for you to change your wording during your presentation if things don't go the way you anticipated. Memorization is a dangerous strategy that can stand as a barrier between you and your audience.

Delivering Speech in Natural Voice

If you sound fake or too perfect, you are going to miss the chance to connect with your audience or break whatever connection they already have with you. Generally, you should only speak in a conversational manner. If you catch yourself speaking with some 'ahs' and 'ums,' you shouldn't fidget as it is not anything you have to worry about. Just try to be natural.

Voice Modulations

If, as a speaker, you hope to be more engaging, you should avoid talking in a way that makes it look like you have rehearsed your speech a little too much. This does not mean that you should not pick up with your pace and inflection while you deliver your speech and as you are practicing.

To deliver in the appropriate rhythm, you should record yourself while practicing and then listen to the record at a later time. By doing this, you will be able to take note of the points where you sounded inauthentic. With your natural voice, it is still very possible for you to make use of the appropriate modulations.

Being Short and Precise

Regardless of the amount of time given to you to deliver your speech, try to keep it short. You do not have to use all the time you were given. Pass all the information you need to pass and make use of the time left for questioning, or you can dismiss your audience earlier that you ordinarily should.

Your goal during a speech is to try to pass your point or a piece of information across, and you may not need a whole hour to do this, so when you think you have achieved your goal, you can simply conclude and drop the mic. You need to ensure that your audience can take in and process your speech more easily, so if it is possible for you to do so in as little as 15 minutes, by all means, do so and make use of the remaining time to satisfy the curiosity of your audience.

In a research conducted by Dianne Dukette and David Cornish in 2009, it was discovered that humans are only able to maintain attention for an average of about 20 minutes and that the short-term response to a stimulus that helps them to pay attention to a particular thing lasts for just a few seconds. What this means is that when you appear before a crowd, you only have about eight seconds to arrest their attention. Also, this means that a presentation that lasts for more than 20 minutes needs to be broken into smaller bits, with about 20 minutes per session.

Bonding with Audience

When you give a speech, treat it like a conversation. This means that you will need to pass the message you have in mind to the other person(s). For this, it does not matter if you have a large or small audience. The problem lies with the mere fact that everyone is subject to a large amount of information in a short time, so as a speaker, it may be a bit difficult for you to filter through all the distractions and assure your audience that you have something important to tell them.

As you speak, it is possible that people have their phones, laptops, or tablets to deal with because they are busy replying to emails, surfing the internet, or trying to figure out who you are. They may even be taking notes on their gadgets from what you are saying, but it is your role to captivate them enough to make them want to drop their devices and listen to what you are saying. You cannot possibly ask them to turn their phones off, but you can make them forget their phones by making room for an exciting and engaging atmosphere for the listeners.

Below are some tips on how to connect with your audience:
- Tell them stories
- Keep your target audience in mind
- Be aware of the energy in the room
- Be willing to poke fun at yourself occasionally
- Develop an effective body language

Storytelling

Being a good storyteller is one of the best ways to engage your audience. This is an important point in public speaking that one cannot simply neglect it, and it can also not be overemphasized. It is a reliable tool that some of the best speakers in history have used to connect with their audience. This technique is used to build an atmosphere that allows the audience to listen to the speaker more easily. It makes the audience to feel like the speaker is not trying to shove information at them with the hope that they are going to remember the information that is being passed.

The best and the most enjoyable presentations are ones that don't feel like presentations but stories that are told by people who have exciting experiences to share. These stories may be tales of your own experiences, or they may be classic stories that can help your audience relate to your presentation in a particular context. Take most of the popular/most influential TED Talks, for example. Most of them are influenced by stories, and this is one of the reasons why they stand out.

If you must tell a story, ensure that your story is relatable, understandable, and easy to retell. With communication as a medium, stories are always very easy to stick to the minds of people, so when you are writing your speech, consider the things that you have to see to enable you to set a context which your audience is going to understand and engage with.

Repetition

Repetitions are used to ensure that your listeners leave the venue with the focal point of your presentation. It helps to make sure that you are clear and helps with encouraging the audience to embrace the idea.

To be able to make use of effective repetitions in your presentation, you have to figure out what the main point of your presentation, which you hope will stick to the minds of your audience. During your presentation, keep saying these points so that in case they missed it the last time you said it, they are going to get it as you have said it again.

Constant Practice

Have you ever heard a person say that he wishes to remain authentic during a speech, but they don't want to practice their speech beforehand? Though this may appear to be a bit contradictory, the truth is that the more you practice your speech, the more you can gain spontaneity during the actual presentation. All you need to do is to ensure that you practice the right way.

Make sure that during every practice, you can put your environment into consideration, so you practice as though there is an audience in front of you as you are practicing. Don't make the mistake of brushing through your presentation while on transit, as this will more likely do you more harm than good.

By practicing, you will feel more confident, and you will look more authentic. Therefore, you will create a good chance to connect with your listeners. In the end, you will be able to achieve the ultimate goal of public speaking, which is building a connection with your audience.

Chapter 6: Influencing People

Are you an employer who needs to make sure every employee are on the same page, a customer relations officer who need to answer all the queries of customers, a sales representative who need to convince customers to purchase a product or one who simply has to make sure that the kids do their home works? One sure thing is that it is not always easy to get people to change their minds. The ability to do this relies on powerful skills and your ability to influence people. While you strive to influence people, you have to be careful not to cross the thin line between influencing and manipulation.

Influencing is totally different from manipulation. Influence is your ability to affect the behavior, character, and the development of people or on something. Using influence means you get to affect someone directly or indirectly in an important way. A person that is being influenced can be aware of the motive of the influencer. With manipulation, that is different. Manipulation involves controlling someone to your advantage.

At one point or the other in the life of everyone, we have been faced with the need to influence others, but for most of us, there is a need to learn how to do this better. This may be at work or in our everyday lives, and the need for this skill may arise in either big or small situations. For most people, there is a genuine need/intention to influence people and not manipulate them.

You may be tempted to ask what the difference between influence and manipulation is because you wish to know how you can possibly differentiate between the two. Also, you want to know you can realize when you are crossing the line. The absolute truth to this is that to influence without manipulation is a process.

Influence can be said to be one's ability to persuade a person to think the way we want. This is a very important life skill in all works of life. As a matter of fact, a person who is not able to convince people can never boast of excellent leadership skills. As a leader, it is very important to understand the art of influencing others. By so doing, he/she will use this understanding as a tool for becoming more skilled in getting things done.

Influencing people is one thing that leaders do at every level with different people. Every human being tries to influence almost all the people they come across in different ways. This may manifest in trying to convince a person to like/accept you or trying to get them to leave you alone. It may also be in getting others to sign a petition or getting them to give thoughts to certain systems.

Important Qualities to Possess To Influence people

Influence isn't something you can achieve through coercion and intimidating people; it is from within. Your ability to motivate and inspire people around you is your influence.

Influence
is Power!

Becoming a charismatic person requires that you master the art of influence. Being influential has nothing to do with gaining popularity or gathering titles; it is about obtaining the confidence, trust, and admiration of people around you. Influence is also about how you engage other people, and how your vision attracts people to you. It may seem difficult to nail down precisely how a person exactly influences others. However, there are some unique qualities that influencers possess before they can be referred to as influencers. Let's take a look at some of those qualities.

A Unique Drive and Hunger

Hunger and drive are two qualities that help differentiate between a leader and a follower. Leaders are always on a quest to get things done. They always feel like they must create, do, or share. This drive is the force that makes leaders unstoppable. This drive is what makes them realize how they can influence people.

If you look closely at the lives of the most successful leaders in the history of mankind, you will notice how they can get their hunger from a variety of sources, but most times, it comes from a particular point of lack in their lives. You will also notice that they all have an interest in confronting authorities. They are the type of people who are not afraid to challenge an old order by not conforming to mediocrity. As a leader, there is a need to influence people, and to do this, you have to look out for anything that will intensify the hunger and drive that lies within you. The greatest hunger is in service to something that is within you.

An Exceptional and Compelling Vision

There is little or no power in small visions as they cannot easily inspire or move you, and they will not help you to reach your full potentials or explore your abilities. Instead of influencing others, when you have a small vision, you will find yourself seeking attention and validation, so if you are willing to tap into an extraordinary life, you need to have big dreams. This is the reason why the greatest leaders seem to have visions that are scary and bigger than themselves.

Many leaders make the mistake of trying to influence other people to support a selfish goal. You always have to remind yourself that there is so much power in wielding your influence, so you have to use this power to bring about change for a greater good only. It becomes manipulation when you try to make use of it for selfish reasons, and those whom you are trying to use it for will easily take note of it.

If you must actually stand out and influence others, your vision has to be captivating, such that it will win the hearts, minds, and energy of a large number of people. This must be the vision of the way life can become better for some people, customers, gender, race, or an entire country. There must be that thing that will make people willing to give up their resources and contribute their energy to reach the desired goal. With a specific purpose for the benefit of all, others will become interested and willing to help you to get to your goals, and they will also influence other people to assist you as well.

Absolute Certainty

A charismatic person always has a strong belief in the fact that they can achieve their dreams. There is a lot of power in beliefs, and the way it influences other people begins with a simple conviction. Certainty is something that shapes humans as it is one of the six human needs. It is also a very important part of how you can influence people.

Some of the greatest barriers of trying to influence others lie in doubt, uncertainty, and fear. Certainly, people who are influential know that the fear of not keeping up with their dreams is worse than the fear that is linked with forging ahead. This is the reason why they would rather make use of fear rather than letting it use them.

Consider the most charismatic people you have seen in action. Most times, their passion seems infectious. A charismatic leader will not discourage his team by expressing doubts by saying negative things like: "I don't think we can achieve this goal," or "I am not fit for this job." What a charismatic leader does is to get everyone involved busy by going about his business with absolute certainty. Their fear is what they use to push themselves and those around them harder, and this will go a long way in helping them to influence other people.

A Passionate and Good Communicator

To influence others, you must find out those things that already influence them. This way, it will become easy for you to influence them and make the desired/real change. You will need to understand your audience and the way you can get to your audience. Your passion is what brings the energy to the room, and to be effective, and you have to know who your listeners are and how you are going to speak with them in a way that is going to move them. Everyone has a particular thing that drives them, so you have to discover the right one. This is very important.

Most of the people who are trying to influence others make the mistake of communicating with a style that works for them. Except if you get lucky and are in the midst of those that think the way you think, this communication style may fail. People who are good at influencing people to understand that knowing their audience better is important for communication, and you cannot influence another without effective communication. With passionate and effective communication, you will be able to summon the required energy for inspiring others to do something that may not be considered as normal. It may as well be something extraordinary.

Intelligent Strategists

Exceptional, charismatic leaders who can bring about change, have a strategy. This strategy is a technique or a way of moving ahead from their previous position to the place they wish to be to be able to live their dreams. Though they may not be what may be considered as natural strategists, they know how they can easily spot a strategy that will be of help, and they make use of this strategy for their own purpose.

Charismatic people who can influence people always make use of strategic communication styles and messaging. They employ strategies in the way a job is going to be done and how they can easily work with a group of people. They know the strategy they can employ for their actions, as well as a strategy for communication. If you must influence others, you will need to know the point when it is necessary to give and when you must receive or demand. You should know when you can talk and when you have to be quiet and listen with undivided attention. Although developing strategies deals with coming up with an action plan, it also deals with knowing the point when those around you need recuperation. As you are trying to create a strategy, you should never hesitate to re-evaluate your actions.

Being Able to Connect, Care, and Break Patterns

If you must make the needed change and influence other people, you have to break a particular trend. Charismatic leaders are aware of this fact, and they make use of it in challenging people. Note, the way people challenge others is different.

While some may choose to make use of humor to change the patterns, others do so by paying keen attention and also being empathetic to others. All of them have something in common, and that is the fact that they actually care about the people they are influencing and the way they connect with those people. When you care enough about someone to connect with them and also gain knowledge of their ways, you will be able to influence them. Without this very important knowledge, you may be using the wrong mode of communication, which is not effective in influencing other people, and you may not find out why.

One of the reasons why this skill is important for every charismatic leader is because you may encounter a group or a person who is going to hamper your progress. You will also need to find ways of influencing those that have beliefs that are limiting them by holding them away from being able to break their pattern and show them to another path entails that you are going to need to be very powerful.

Ability to Set Unrealistic Standards and Expectations

To be able to influence other people and bring about change, you have to come up with a standard or expectations that are not realistic. If something must happen for a change, you have to ensure that you do not settle, and you will also know how to influence other people not to settle as well. Typically, it is those things that we tolerate that will come to us. As people with charisma, we have to build a culture that will help people to live bigger lives with bigger expectations of the things they can do and the way they should be treated.

Maybe the most visible difference between a manager and a leader who influences other people is the fact that a manager makes sure people do things under his supervision. As for a leader, he inspires others to set new standards, including when the leader is not available. The reason why people continue to live according to new rules is that the new rules have also become their standard. Unrealistic expectations are what change the world, and in cases where leaders have higher standards and know how they can influence other people to accept these higher standards, innovations, and lasting change takes place.

The Courage and Faith to Take Actions

Being courageous means that even though you are afraid of a task, you are going to do it regardless. Having faith, on the other hand, means that you are going to work towards a challenging goal because you have a firm belief in the fact that acts for a greater good. There are people who can tap into these two, and they also know how they can influence others to embrace this same courage and faith. This does not mean that leaders do not harbor fear or experience it at all; what it means that they know how to use it to their favor rather than allowing it to destroy their lives.

Consider the difference between faith and fear. The truth is that these two are made up of ideas. While fear is an imagination that is not directed, faith is an imagination that is consciously directed for a greater good. Exceptional leaders understand this idea, and they know the best ways to make use of it to influence other people. They dare to take calculated risks with faith that, in a way, though it may be a bit of a challenge, they are going to have the courage to get back on track if they fail. This ideology is what motivates other people to move along with their fears and creates a kind of effect that brings about lasting change.

A Persistent but Flexible Approach

Charismatic leaders never miss the chance to learn with every interaction and every event. They never turn their backs to their innate ability to adapt to new environments or cultivate new habits/skills. Within them is a hunger to garner everything that they can to master everything that can be linked to their vision.

With a very incredible level of persistence, they can turn their setbacks into successes, and this is one of the reasons why they can easily become very influential.

Recall that persistence does not in any way mean that you have to be rigid. A charismatic person is flexible, and this is what allows him to make the required change whenever things are not going the way they anticipate. Failure cannot possibly stop them because out of every seeming failure, and they can pick a lesson. You have to consider it this way, though you are persistent in getting the desired outcome, your approach towards achieving the goal is flexible.

People who wish to influence others normally make the mistake of being rigid in their quest for mastering persistence. They remain fixed in pursuing that goal or engage in that activity that they have engaged in from the very beginning, even though their actions do not seem to be yielding results. Therefore, you have to remember that your persistence is going to have counter effects if you don't match it up with flexibility.

Authentic and Coherence

Remember that a good leader will always have to strive to lead by example. Every time he is trying to influence others, they always ensure that their actions match their words. They will not be caught asking other people to do things that they do not want to do or things that they haven't already done by themselves. While leading from their most important values, they are aware of the fact that it is meaningless to try to influence others if it does not come from an authentic part of them. If you must have credibility, authenticity is one thing you must have, and you must always stay in line with the things you say and the things you do. It is not possible to lead or attain success if you are not credible in your quest for ways of influencing other people.

Every great leader and everyone who has mastered the art of influencing others has unique stories of endless possibilities rather than impossibilities. You cannot be considered as a leader if you are prone to telling stories of impossibilities or stories of how you are not going to be able to achieve something. These types of people have already lost hope from the beginning.

How to Influence People

If you are looking at it on the surface, influence can be considered as compliance, which is in a person's ability to get others to do what they want. Ideally, one has to show a genuine commitment to other people to accomplish the most important goals and tasks.

In the early phase of one's career or while delivering on your roles as a contributor to a task, influence will mean your ability to work effectively with other people who you do not have any authority on. It demands that you engage in logical and compelling arguments. You will also have to be a giver, as much as you are a taker. When you occupy a senior position or an executive role, your goal as regards influencing people will have to be focused on ways of setting the pace for long-range objectives, inspiration, as well as motivation.

Whichever position you occupy in a group or an organization, there is a possibility that you wish to master tactics that will help you to influence others as this is one of the most important skills for a leader. Generally, influencing falls under three broad categories, to understand the act of influencing, you have to consider the following:

The three categories of influencing include logical, emotional, and cooperative appeals. These are also known as influencing the head, hearts, and hands.

Logical Appeal

This is the ability of an individual to tap into the rational and intellectual stance of other people. To do this, you have to bring an argument forward, to determine the most preferred choice of action for the benefits of an organization, an individual, or both the organization or the individual. This largely has to do with appealing to the minds of others.

Emotional Appeal

This has to do with a person's ability to connect his message, goal, or his project to the goals and the values of an individual. It deals with a particular idea that boosts a person's emotion in terms of his wellbeing, service, or his sense of belonging. This will affect the other person's heart, and it will give the influencer a greater chance of gaining the support of his target.

Cooperative Appeal

This is a method of influencing collaboration. It has to do with what people can achieve together, consultation by seeking out the ideas that other people have, and the alliances that can be formed with others in terms of those whose support you already have and those who are credible enough to give you the support you need. By working together to achieve an important goal that everyone has agreed on, you give a hand to other people in your circle, and this will go a long way in influencing them.

Below are simple ways to put these tactics into practice:

- **Give Them the Things They Want**

If you must influence people, you should be ready to give them the things they desire. This is because there is a bit of selfishness in everyone, so they will naturally like the things they want as opposed to the ones you want. So for a moment, set yourself aside and think about the other person. When you think of others and the things that they need, they will begin to perceive you as a great person, fall in love with you, give you more respect and bestow more authority on you. This is simple logic because people think more about themselves, you will be able to influence them if they feel like you are thinking about them too by giving them the things that they want.

- **Make Other People Feel like They Matter to You**

If you make them feel important, people will do whatever you need them to do for you. This is a very important factor in the act of influencing others. Everyone likes the feeling that comes with feeling important, and you also like it too.

When you make others feel important, they are very likely to want to stand by you. This will help you to get them to do the things you want them to do, except if your goals are in line with theirs and they already want to do what you want them to do, so it is not your influence that got them to do what they want to do. If, for example, you ask a cleaner to sweep the floor, he will do it, but he may not be passionate about it because it is likely that he is only doing it for the pay. If on the other hand, you tell them that they are important to you because, without them, your space won't be neat and tidy, they will become more passionate about cleaning, and they will love you for your attitude.

- **Connect with People's Emotions**

You will not need to ask people to do things for you if you can connect with their emotions because they will most likely willingly do things for you. Try to become more understanding by connecting your emotions with theirs. This is one way to place you in the position of a leader by helping you to influence them.

For instance, if you run a company, your company will thrive more if you can build a connection between the emotions of those who are working for you and the goals of your company. If you can successfully do this, you will find that your employees will be willing to do whatever they can to help you to achieve your desired goal.

- **Empower Them**

You will be considered as a better leader with more authority if you can empower other people. What you need to do is to give them the necessary motivation to empower them.

As Maya Angelou once said, people will easily forget the things you said, they will forget the things you did, but they will not forget the way you made them feel. If you can empower people, you will be some steps closer to influencing them. Most successful people can empower those that work with them, and this is the reason why they easily become great influencers.

If you are willing to become more powerful and a better influencer, you have to begin with empowering them, with time, you will begin to see changes.

- **Respect the Opinion of Others**

Never make it your duty to tell other people that they are wrong. You should also respect their opinion even when you don't believe in them because they are allowed to have different beliefs. From their perspective, they will think that they are right, and that is okay.

If someone tells you something you consider wrong, do not outrightly tell them that they are wrong. You can make them understand that though you respect their opinion, you see things quite differently and ask them if they wish to know why you think the way you do. If they wish to know why you think differently, then you have a tour chance of bearing your mind to them without having to offend them or hurt their ego. If you wish to influence people, this is the best way to go.

- **Rather Than Being a Boss, Be a Leader**

Typically, leaders are people who can work with others on projects by sharing a collective vision and goal. While working with others, he ensures that he does not order them around.

A boss, on the other hand, is one who orders people around to do the thing he needs to do, and he does not coordinate others. To be able to influence others, you have to be a leader who can empower others and coordinate them.

Being a boss will not help you become influential. It would rather ruin every chance you have to influence others. Being bossy will only make your co-workers say bad and terrible things behind your back. When you are a leader, they will say good things about you even when you are not around. A good influencer is one who can communicate well with those whom he is working with.

- **Show Sympathy**

Do not scold people when you notice that they are making a mistake. You always have to remember that they are also humans. Humans will naturally make mistakes, but if you really care about them, you are going to need to help them not to repeat their mistakes.

If you wish to influence others, you will need to tell them specifically in a way that will help them gain a better understanding of your point, without getting hurt.

The best way to tell people that they have made a mistake is to find common ground. Tell them that you have also made the same mistake in the past. This will make room for mutual understanding born out of sympathy. By doing this, people will easily understand you more.

The trick is in telling them that though you have made the same mistake, you were able to learn not to repeat your mistakes, so you hope/believe that they are not going to make a mistake again.

- **Choose Your Target Wisely**

Your target has to be a person in whom you can fill a void and someone to whom you have something to offer. This may be a PR manager, a potential client, or a boss who has the power to give you that much-needed promotion. You should not focus your energy on influencing people that are anxious to please you because most times, they are hoping that they will get something from you. You should rather look at influencing those that give subtle clues like shyness when they see you. These are the type of people whom you can actually influence.

- **Approach Them Directly By Creating a Sense of Security in Them**

If you wish to click with a very influential member of an executive board, or a potential client, for instance, you will find yourself at risk of making them raise their guard against you if you demand something from them as soon as you meet them. Before making your request, get a third party to approach them or try to build a neutral or a friendly relationship with them before you make the relationship about business.

- **Show Mixed Signals**

Once you can hook someone, create an air of mystery to keep that person's interest arrested. If you are meeting a person that has a professional network that you are willing to gain access to, try to make yourself look like an intellectual and appear sophisticated but chip in sarcastic comments or funny comments that contributes to the depth of your character.

- **Appear As Something That Should Be Desired**

Do you know how a multitude of people lusts over celebrities? Clients or customers will naturally be attracted to the most appealing companies or managers. Do not make a fool of yourself by bringing yourself too low in your quest for winning people over to yourself. Flaunt those connections, achievements, and successes that you are most fond of.

- **Create a Need By Stirring Anxiety and Discontent**

You cannot easily seduce people if they are not content. Sell a good image of yourself by highlighting how the other person does not match up to you in a way and then show how you will be able to make up for the things they lack. You can also prove how a client is wasting money in a business and suggests a few changes that can possibly change the company for the better.

Chapter 7: Effect of Charisma on Successful Leadership

Successful people are typically leaders who can get those around them to assist them in achieving their goals. Getting people to work with you in achieving your goals is always much easier than done. Leaders are very important parts of the human race as they are the ones that have the strength and courage to get people to work according to certain beliefs to get them to support the things that they are doing and get them to reach where they need to be. The reason why people are likely to get you to get to the point where you need to be is the reason why you are doing what you are doing, and not what you are doing itself.

Good communication skills are one important part of charismatic leadership, and charismatic leaders are often those leaders that are verbally eloquent, such that they can communicate with their followers on a deep and emotional level. They can translate a very compelling vision into words to draw strong emotions from their followers. This is one of the reasons why they are always successful leaders. Take Steve Jobs, for example, and he didn't achieve everything on his own. He had the skills of the most talented people to help him get to where he was, and these people believed strongly in his dreams and were able to get him to achieve success because of his uniqueness and charisma.

Charisma is that thing that illuminates the room as you walk in. It is about the qualities of an individual, which elicits a feeling in others in a way that others can't. Charisma enables one to make valuable impacts and makes others listen to you as though you are a god on earth whenever you speak. Though some people are naturally charismatic, it is possible to learn or develop these qualities and put them into action as though it is something you came to live with.

The reason why charismatic people always seem to be successful is because they have the eye of an eagle and an omnipotent personality that is still able to connect with people and empathize with others and also make them feel important as everyone else in the room. Below are some of the qualities of charismatic people that helps them to be successful in leadership:

Increased Loyalty from Employees

As a result of the fact that charismatic leaders are always keen on motivating and inspiring their employees, there is a lot of likelihood that their leadership skills can inform an increase in loyalty and commitment levels from their employees. Most of the time, they ensure that their employees are able to feel like their efforts and talents matter. This is one of the factors that increase employee engagement and decrease employee turnover.

Charismatic Leaders Create Leaders

Leaders and managers who are charismatic also have an infectious personality that can easily motivate young employees to become leaders in the long run. The unique qualities of this type of leader will go down the radar to form a large part of an employee's management style when he/she also gets to a position of leadership.

Increased Productivity

These types of leaders are highly skilled in the act of gaining the trust of those that are around them, so there are greater chances of employees sticking to the expectations of their charismatic leaders, no matter how high it may seem. This, as a result, constitutes a high probability of bringing about increased productivity, as well as a better quality of work.

A Shot at Innovation

Charismatic leaders are prone to making positive change and innovations that seem logical. This is the reason why they are always in search of ways of getting better opportunities that will have a positive effect on the organization and also make processes easy. As a result of this, the company will always be kept abreast of the latest trends in the industry, as well as the latest organizational practices.

A Learning Culture

Humility is one of the most important characteristics of a charismatic leader. Others are good communication skills, as well as self-improvement. As a result of the fact that this type of leaders set their eyes on growth, they can consider consequences and mistakes as opportunities to learn. They encourage their subordinates to find other solutions to their problems when their initial plans do not work as anticipated. This will create an atmosphere where employees will be more comfortable to take risks and seek better solutions to their problems.

Charismatic Leaders Pass for Great Listeners

People sometimes underestimate the power of listening. It does not only make people feel like they are important to you, but it also helps you to understand what the person has to say and know what the person's point of view is. If you don't listen, you won't be able to know the thoughts of others. By asking appropriate questions, making eye contact, gestures, and body language, you can show to others that they have your undivided attention. This is everything that contributes to making charismatic people good communicators.

They understand that there are things that they should not say, and they know what they should say in many situations. This is one great leadership skill that they possess. They also understand that when they listen to others, they will be able to win them over because they have gained the ability to make them feel special.

They Are Good Observers

There is also so much power in observing things, and this is one of the tools that charismatic leaders arm themselves with. Observation means that you are taking note of all the things that are happening around you as the actions of your employees, the setting of the workplace, the energy people are carrying around, the most important people in the gathering and the things that are actually happening asides the artificial essence of the gathering.

There are a lot of people who are able to see, but they lack vision. Charismatic people take note of everything, and they watch everything keenly. It may be almost impossible to get them to move past something without taking notes or move something over them without their notice. This is because they are very obsessed with knowing the details of everything. As a result of this, it will be difficult for things to go wrong under their watch because they are going to notice the moment things start getting suspicious.

In an incredible manner, charismatic leaders walk around as though they have a telescope inserted into their eyes. Before they engage in an activity or take action on an issue, they study it by watching it keenly. This will help them to prepare for whichever situation that may arise.

Charismatic Leaders Know the Right Time and Place for Everything

Considering that there are a whole lot of distractions in the modern world, charismatic leaders can maintain their respect for other people. You will not easily catch them pressing their phones when they are seated in front of another person, and they will not also easily get distracted by focusing their attention on something that is not very important. This is a very important gift that very few people possess and give to their audience. This is one of the gifts that earns charismatic leaders respect and makes people want to be with them. People also remember them for this and will also wish to work for them more.

Charismatic Leaders are Selflessness

Charismatic leaders understand clearly that there is no giving without getting so they do not just focus on the things that they are going to get out of something, someone, or a situation. They would rather focus on the things that they can give for those around them and the entire universe. Charismatic leaders are well aware of the fact that their input reflects directly on the result they get.

Charismatic Leaders Don't Place So Much Importance on Themselves

Though charismatic people can easily come off as cocky, confident, and a little bit arrogant, they also understand that there are certain lines that they must not cross, and one of those lines is acting as if they are very important or a big shot. This may rub off on others as a very cheap show-off, and this is common with people with low self-esteem as they always want to receive credit for things to paint a good picture of themselves. These types of people are not difficult to identify.

It is only people who also have low self-esteem and are pretentious that they can appreciate these types of people, and as a charismatic person, you will not want to be described as such. Most right-thinking people will not be impressed by such acts, and they may even become uncomfortable. Your insecurities are causing you to want to show off. Charismatic leaders will not easily want to cross this line because they do not want to become the first enemy of those whom they should have as allies.

They Identify the Fact That Others Are Also Important

It is no news that Rome was not built in a day, and it was not also built by a single person. You are not an island, so you are definitely going to need other people to get to the desired end. Charismatic leaders understand this, and not only are they open to learning from others, but they also use the lessons learned in their favor. These types of leaders know that it is not about the number of people in their camps but their quality and the value they have, so they hold every member of their camp to very high esteem. These days, you do not only need knowledge, but you also need people.

Charismatic Leaders Are Humble

The greatest leaders in history are ones who were able to inspire others to act, and they do this by acknowledging others and giving them credit. They are also humble people who never forget where they came from. They also never try too hard to impress others. They rely on their actions to speak for them, where others rely on their words to do the same.

This is the point where there is a gap between mediocrity and greatness. They commend those that are doing well to encourage them to perform better. With humility, they can create emotional bonds between themselves and their teams instead of just building work relationships with them or forming intellectual relationships with them. They understand that they should never come off as being too proud because excessive pride is the breeding ground for envy and hatred within their organization.

Charismatic Leaders are Visionaries

Charismatic leaders always work with a target. They are well aware of where they are headed or where they wish to be. By being clear about their vision, they can work hard to achieve it. The vision of charismatic leaders is not just clear visions but compelling ones that are in line with their core values, their interests, and their desires.

Charismatic leaders display a kind of passion for their vision that is so strong that it gets others to also believe in their visions. This vision connects to the deepest interests of the leader and those around him, such that it triggers them to reach their highest potentials. It is a type of vision that will help you to know the reasons why you are doing the things you are doing, regardless of the things that are happening outside of the individual and the challenges that come at you at any point.

Charismatic Leaders Always Carry Positive Energy

You will always take note of a charismatic person the moment they step into the room. There is something about them that makes them carry a kind of energy that not everybody has. They are light-bearers, and once they step, the whole rooms become interested in the things that they have to say. This is as a result of their charisma. With this, they can entertain everyone in the room and can get along with anyone they decide to get along with.

This is a very important quality that helps them to carry others along by leading them. People are naturally attracted to strong and passionate personalities. This type of passion and energy helps them to cultivate a type of personality that brings about admiration and ideologies that others can aspire to. This is also known as the ideal ego.

Charismatic Leaders Inspire Others

There is a popular saying that states that it is not what a person does but the reason why he does it. Charismatic leaders inspire others to take action and encourage them to believe in the things that they do as they serve as motivation that will help them to achieve their dreams/goals. Charismatic people encourage others to believe in their goals and dreams as well as inspire them to pursue a greater purpose. Above all, they try to make everyone around them feel special as an important part of the team's journey to greatness, rather than just treat them as mere employees.

Conclusion

Since you have read to this point, I am quite certain that you are not the same as you were when you started reading this book, and we are glad that I have been able to make a difference.

In the beginning, we stated how the need to influence people is very dormant in every human, and we have taken you through the journey of satisfying that need as a leader and as a good public speaker. In this book, I have described what it means to be an influential and charismatic leader. Confidence plays a very important role in the quest for being charismatic, and one of the best ways to show this is through public speaking.

While there are some people, who are not very good at speaking before a crowd while some others are very good at captivating an audience with their public speaking skills, when it comes to addressing an audience, there are some important things that a person should learn to do. Those are the things that make some people better public speakers than others. These skills also contribute largely to helping one become influential.

In leadership, both charisma and influence are very important as they work together to determine the success of a leader. It is important to note that leadership is about those that are under you, much more than it is about you. For this reason, you need a lot of emotional intelligence and empathy to be a successful leader. This also requires charisma and a conscious effort to do better as a leader. To do this, you have to get into the minds of your target and try to know the way they feel. This will go a long way to help you make the most out of leadership.

In a nutshell, this book is an embodiment of everything you need to know about being influential, confident, and charismatic. We hope you have enjoyed it.